THE
ANARCHIST

THE ANARCHIST

A PLAY BY **DAVID MAMET**

THEATRE COMMUNICATIONS GROUP   NEW YORK   2012

The Anarchist is published by Theatre Communications Group, Inc., 520 Eighth Avenue, 24th Floor, New York, NY 10018-4156

The publication of *The Anarchist* by David Mamet, through TCG's Book Program, is made possible in part by the New York State Council on the Arts with the support of Governor Andrew Cuomo and the New York State Legislature.

TCG books are exclusively distributed to the book trade by Consortium Book Sales and Distribution.

Cataloging-in-Publication Data is on file at the Library of Congress, Washington, D.C.

ISBN: 978-1-55936-412-6

Book design and composition by Lisa Govan
Cover art and design by aka

First Edition, December 2012

This play is dedicated to Patti and Debra

Chaque génération doit dans une relative opacité
découvrir sa mission, la remplir ou trahir.

— Frantz Fanon
Les damnés de la terre

PRODUCTION HISTORY

The Anarchist premiered on Broadway on December 2, 2012, at the John Golden Theatre (Producers: Jeffrey Richards; Jerry Frankel; Howard and Janet Kagan; Catherine Schreiber; Jam Theatricals; Luigi and Rose Caiola; Gutterman Chernoff MXKC; Kit Seidel; Broadway Across America; Amy and Phil Mickelson; James Fuld, Jr.; Carlos Arana/Bard Theatricals; Will Trice). The production was directed by David Mamet, with scenic and costume design by Patrizia Von Brandenstein, lighting design by Jeff Croiter and sound design by Peter Fitzgerald; the production stage manager was William Joseph Barnes. The cast was:

CATHY	Patti LuPone
ANN	Debra Winger

CHARACTERS

Cathy and Ann, two women

SCENE

An office

Ann, seated at a desk. A telephone is on the desk. An intercom sits on a conference table. Also on the desk are several files, a loosely bound manuscript and several books. A briefcase sits on the floor. Cathy is standing.

ANN: Will you sit down? How are you?
CATHY: No, I think I'm well. Thank you for asking.
ANN: What have you been doing?
CATHY: I've been studying. As usual.
ANN: And what have you learned?
CATHY: In the larger sense . . .
ANN: . . . all right.
CATHY: I hope that I've learned to be reasonable. At least I have studied it. Most importantly.
ANN: *Most* importantly.
CATHY: Yes.
ANN: *Reason* more than patience?
CATHY: One might think the pressing study would be patience. But patience, of course, implies an end.
ANN: "Patience implies an end."
CATHY: Well, yes.
ANN: As?

CATHY: One may be patient only *for* something.

ANN: Such as?

CATHY: A deferred *desire*, or the cessation of *discomfort* . . .

ANN: Revenge?

CATHY: Well, that would fall within the rubric of desire deferred.

ANN: And Reason teaches?

CATHY: *Reason* would teach the abandonment of the unfulfill-able wish; and, so, of the need for patience. It therefore may be said to be the higher study.

(Cathy gestures back, toward upstage. Pause.)

Lovely girl.

ANN: Yes?

CATHY: In the anteroom. *(Pause)* I find when conversation stalls it never indicates a want of subject—one may always talk about the weather—but rather some subject's repression. What is it?

ANN: I'm leaving.

CATHY: Yes, we were expecting that announcement quite some time. Well. *(Pause)* Everything ends. That is neither a new nor a monumental understanding. But it's true.

ANN *(Points to the large manuscript on her desk)*: I've been read-ing your book.

CATHY: Is it a book?

ANN: Isn't it?

CATHY: Well. You are the first to read it.

ANN: I'm honored.

CATHY: And, you know, I've been thinking of it, so long, as a . . .

ANN: . . . "A" . . . ?

CATHY: A manuscript, a "work-in-progress" . . . A "collection of . . ."

ANN: Why would that not be a book?

CATHY: No, I'll take your comment as an endorsement. Thank you.

ANN: You're welcome, Cathy.

CATHY: If it is a book, it remains only to see what a publisher . . . And what the Public, but, of course, I am ahead of myself.

ANN: No, of course it's a book . . . (*Picks up the manuscript and reads*) "When he came. The first time. He questioned me."

CATHY: . . . oh, yes . . .

ANN (*Reading*): "And I said, in answer to him, 'I revere Jesus, though I do not worship him. But I have the utmost respect, and I might say "love," for those who do.'" It's quite beautiful.

CATHY: You chose that phrase purposefully.

ANN: In order to?

CATHY: To compliment me.

ANN: No. But I would have. As with much of the book.

CATHY: Thank you.

ANN: And that was the first meeting.

CATHY: What was the first meeting?

ANN: You describe here . . .

CATHY: With?

ANN: The priest.

CATHY: The meeting with the priest?

ANN: Yes?

CATHY: The first time? I don't know if that was it. But some time. During that first year.

ANN: In the first year yes.

CATHY: Not regularly. He came, of course, as part of the rotation.

ANN: The rabbi also came, during that time.

CATHY: That's right, and the Protestant . . .

ANN: Yes.

CATHY: . . . minister. The word is *minister*. (*Pause*) I forgot a French verb yesterday.

ANN: The minister.

CATHY: Came regularly.

ANN: Would you like some coffee.

CATHY: No, thank you.

ANN: Did they give you breakfast.

CATHY: I wasn't hungry. (*Pause*) "Who came when." Poor clerks. Copying Notations in the Logs, no one would see.

ANN: I saw them.

CATHY: I meant no disrespect.

ANN: I understand.

(Pause. Then, simultaneously:)

CATHY: How is your daughter?   ANN: And during that time . . .

CATHY: I'm sorry, go ahead.

ANN: Thank you. And, during that time, you also met with the rabbi.

CATHY: I met with them all.

ANN: But, particularly?

CATHY: The rabbi. Why "particularly?"

ANN: Because.

CATHY: Some people. Are born. Into a tradition. In which they perhaps feel other-than-comfortable.

ANN: They . . .

CATHY: Or, better, they, later in life, may discover a covenant, in which, for the first time, they find comfort.

ANN: A covenant? . . .

CATHY: A *home*. A mate. Or a profession. People, late in life, for example, may discover their true *sexuality*, or . . . the parallels are obvious. Mine dealt with Faith.

ANN: Your?

CATHY: Revelation.

ANN: . . . your revelation.

CATHY: Of Christ.

ANN: But you continued . . . *(She consults notes)* During the first years, to meet with the rabbi.

CATHY: That's right.

ANN: After you had discovered this new Covenant.

CATHY: Do you know? I didn't want to insult him.

ANN: Really . . .

CATHY: The others came so seldom. And the rabbi was additionally . . .

ANN: Yes?

CATHY: A sort of "entertainment," faute de mieux. *(Pause)* I forgot a French verb. Yesterday.

ANN: And you were reading . . . ?

CATHY: Actually, I was writing.

ANN: In French.

CATHY: Yes.

ANN: What were you writing?

CATHY: An attempt at a Translation.

ANN: Of your book.

CATHY: Oh very good.

ANN: That's right?

CATHY: Yes.

ANN: An *attempt* at a translation. But you speak French.

CATHY: I did. *(Pause)* Someone asked me, "Do you play an instrument?" I said, "No," with some regret, and then remembered that I played the piano all my life. How about that?

(Pause.)

ANN: You spoke French fluently.

CATHY: As one does. With the vocabulary of one's interests. A sort of "waiter's French."

ANN: And what were your interests?

CATHY: And the language of theology is rather abstruse.

ANN: Your interest, then, was in theology?

CATHY: Well, in hindsight, what else would you call it?

ANN: You were translating your book.

CATHY: I was attempting to.

ANN: And you forgot a verb.

CATHY: I did.

ANN: But you must have had a dictionary.

CATHY: I thought that to use the dictionary, would be admitting, a, a . . . No, I'm getting old. An "unworthiness."

ANN: But, you read widely, in French.

CATHY: Well. That was the Language of the Movement.

ANN: Of the Movement.

CATHY: Yes.

(Pause.)

ANN: Have you read them since? Those books?

CATHY: Those books.

ANN: Yes.

CATHY: Would they be allowed here?

ANN: Well—that's a fair question.

CATHY: But, do you know. I've *thought* about them.

ANN: The books.

CATHY: And, in my *memory*, I couldn't make heads or tails of them.

ANN: *Today*.

CATHY: No. Nor sort out their *attraction*. No, that's not true. They were attractive as they were incendiary.

ANN: "Revolutionary."

CATHY: If you will.

ANN: In their ideas.

CATHY: Not in their *ideas*, no. What *were* they? Finally? *(Pause)* They were essentially a sort of chant.

ANN *(Reads)*: "Words not meant to misdirect are wasted."

CATHY: Well, there you are . . . and their absence of meaning allowed us . . . or, we *understood* them. As a celebration of the transgressive. Because they had no meaning.

(Pause.)

ANN: They wanted Revolution.

CATHY: They?

ANN: The writers.

CATHY: They wanted . . . I suppose.

ANN: And you found it attractive.

CATHY: As the young do. No, it was *thrilling*.

ANN: And now?

(Pause.)

CATHY: They're quite immoral. Don't you think? The French.

ANN: Tell me. Why?

CATHY: They hold the view the world is an illusion.

ANN: Is that their view?

CATHY: Oh, yes. No wonder it sparked terrorism.

ANN: Did it?

CATHY: If nothing has meaning save that we ascribe to it. What reality is there, for example, in another's suffering? As a result of which we find much tragedy. *(Pause)* No wonder they tend to lose wars.

ANN: As in Algeria.

CATHY: Well, yes. *(Pause)* Much tragedy . . .

ANN: As Guillaume's, for example.

CATHY: "Speaking of Algeria."

ANN: That's right.

CATHY: But the meaninglessness—let me be more precise—it was *facing* the meaninglessness which led me to faith.

ANN: It led you to faith.

CATHY: Because, do you see, they're the same two choices.

ANN: The same two as?

CATHY: The bureaucrat and her make-work files. To rebel. Or to submit. And each is unacceptable.

ANN: Is there a third choice?

CATHY: Thank you. And that is the essence of the book.

ANN: That the third choice is Faith.

CATHY: What else could it be? And to believe . . . in the *possibility* of another choice, is to long for God. And to discover it is Faith.

ANN: Faith without certainty.

CATHY: If there were certainty, why would it be Faith?

(Pause.)

ANN: Guillaume had Faith.

CATHY: Faith. Did he?

ANN *(Takes a book from her desk and reads)*: "The growth . . ."

CATHY: He had certainty.

ANN *(Continues reading)*: "The growth of consciousness, causing that pain which may only be . . ." Although a better rendering would be "the growth of *conscience*" don't you think?

CATHY: It's the same word, in French.

ANN: But "conscience" here would be, the better rendering.

CATHY: You may be right. Yes. I think you're right.

ANN: But that was not the translation on the poster.

CATHY: On the poster, no. Not on the poster.

ANN: Quote: "The growth of consciousness, causing that pain, which may only be expunged through violence."

CATHY: That's what the poster said.

ANN: *"Consciousness."*

CATHY: Yes.

ANN: Why?

CATHY: Your point is that a translation as "conscience," that "'conscience' must lead to violence," would have been recognized as absurd.

ANN: That's right.

CATHY: As absurd and monstrous.

ANN: Monstrous, yes.

CATHY: In any case as shocking. Or, say, certainly more *brutal*. The original was shocking.

ANN: And yet.

CATHY: Go on.

ANN: Many were seduced by it.

CATHY: Many were.

ANN: And, I would assume. That it was more seductive in French, which, as you say, is the language of Philosophy.

CATHY: Yes.

ANN: And which additionally carried the romance of being Foreign.

CATHY: Well: to the young, the foreign idea is seductive.

ANN: Why is that?

CATHY: As to the young, everything is foreign. Which is why they are the revolutionaries.

ANN: Because?

CATHY: It's easy. One may easily "make things anew" according to one's insights if one possesses no experience. The French word was "seduire" to seduce.

ANN: "To seduce."

CATHY: "Seduire." And why would I forget it? It's the same word. Funny.

ANN: That was the verb.

CATHY: That's right.

ANN: And you two spoke it.

CATHY: French.

ANN: Yes.

CATHY: Guillaume and I.

ANN: In Algeria.

CATHY: That's right. I wrote of it, in . . .

ANN: No, I've marked it. *(She reads)* "'Ecoute,' he would say, which was, to me, a magic incantation." You say he affected not to understand English.

CATHY: That's right.

ANN: But he did understand.

CATHY: He spoke it perfectly.

ANN: But?

CATHY: He thought it the language of Colonialism.

ANN: More than French.

CATHY: That's right.

ANN: But he was fighting the Colonialism of the French.

CATHY: Well, retrospectively, of course, it's all irrational. And yet they discount Religion. As based on Faith.

(Pause.)

ANN: You wrote in French . . .

CATHY: *Then*.

ANN: Yes.

CATHY: *Did* I . . . ?

ANN: The Speech.

CATHY: . . . in *Algeria* . . .

ANN: And it was quoted.

CATHY: All right.

ANN: And published.

CATHY: *Published*.

ANN: You knew that.

CATHY: I'm not sure I knew it.

ANN: That the speech was published?

CATHY: After the, the . . .

ANN: You knew that. The pamphlet was found. In the apartment.

CATHY: Many things were found in the apartment, which were not mine.

ANN: No. I didn't say the *pamphlet* was yours; I said the speech.

CATHY: The text of the speech.

ANN: Yes.

CATHY: That's right.

ANN: But the pamphlet *could* have been yours, too. It was *essentially* yours.

CATHY: As "the ideas" were mine?

ANN: No. As you "held things in common." Then. Didn't you? You "did not believe in private property"?

(*Pause.*)

CATHY: Oh, my.

ANN: Isn't that what you said? That all pertaining to "the Individual."

CATHY: I . . .

ANN: Even *life* . . .

CATHY: . . . the young are easily corrupted.

ANN: . . . had no personal meaning.

CATHY: No, I.

ANN: That, possessions—like insights—were the property of all. As all was the property of all, and, so, could be taken by any.

CATHY: I . . .

ANN: Meaning you could take it. It was in the speech.

CATHY: Yes. I said that.

ANN: Even Life.

CATHY: I said it.

ANN: Did you believe it?

(*Pause.*)

CATHY: People change.

ANN: Of course.

CATHY: Else . . .

ANN: But did you believe it then?

CATHY: What I did . . .

ANN: Irrespective, of what you did. Tell me. Did you believe it? Truly?

CATHY: I . . .

ANN: That *nothing* was the property of the individual?

CATHY: I don't remember.

(Pause.)

ANN: Do you know, I read the . . . "Pamphlet"?

CATHY: From Algeria.

ANN: "Feuilleton." Pamphlet?

CATHY: Pamphlet. Or leaflet.

ANN: I read it again.

CATHY: Recently.

ANN: I did.

CATHY: I'm surprised one can still find it.

ANN: No. It's still read. Not, perhaps, as it was at the time. Not quite so popular, perhaps. And they still reproduce the Poster.

CATHY: Of Guillaume.

ANN: Though without the quote. Which is, I think, a shame.

CATHY: Why a shame?

ANN: And the "Pamphlet." In anthologies. You must know it.

CATHY: How would I know it?

ANN: The . . . the "statements," your . . .

CATHY: They wouldn't allow the book here.

ANN: No, your "estate" . . . your "royalties" . . .

CATHY: No. I never held the copyright.

ANN: Of course. No. It was for "the People."

CATHY: That's right. Why is it a shame that the quote is not printed on the poster?

ANN: As it might reveal the criminality of worshipping the man.

CATHY: Yes. That's correct.

ANN: And yet, you worshipped him.

CATHY: I did. I was wrong. *(Pause)* I was infatuated with him. Many were.

ANN: Why?

CATHY: Because, in truth: he freed them. That he freed them from those things to which they should perhaps be bound is, you're correct, a different question. The young are uncertain. They're easily frightened. He set them free. And they were grateful. *(Pause)* ". . . he set the people free."

ANN: How are "the People" different from the State?

CATHY: Well, that's the province of philosophy.

ANN: You read philosophy.

CATHY: . . . at *school*.

ANN: No, you were asked. At the time of your arrest, to describe yourself, and you said "a philosopher."

CATHY: . . . all right.

ANN: And on your . . . (*She looks through papers on her desk*) On your Visa application, in French, Profession: "Philosophe." You were quite enamored of the French.

CATHY: We all were.

(*Pause.*)

ANN: He was your lover.

CATHY: He was very beautiful. That's true. Like a beautiful woman, he had *that* power. *You've* seen it. One sees it time to time.

(*Pause.*)

ANN: Are you tired?

CATHY: No. I'm well.

ANN: You said you were well. But the doctor reports lately you've complained of being tired.

CATHY: . . . I'm not tired.

ANN: You said you . . . (*Takes a file and reads it*) "'Felt an illness coming on.' Question: 'Can you say its symptoms?' Answer: 'I don't know. I just feel tired.'"

CATHY: Many people feel that. It's an aspect of age. It has a name.

ANN (*Reads*): "All things have a name. Or they would not exist in our consciousness. If they exist without a name, then we must name them. At whatever cost." Who wrote that?

CATHY: Yes. I wrote it.

ANN: What does it mean?

CATHY: Youth is foolish. Youth can and must be controlled. I've said that.

ANN: For good or ill.

CATHY: As most things.

ANN: And "Youth Unfettered . . ."

CATHY: Yes, all right.

ANN: Finish it. "Youth Unfettered . . ."

CATHY: I do not deny. I've never denied. That I said or that I did those things. Never. *You*. As much as I. Have perhaps done things. In your life. Which you regret.

ANN: What have I done?

CATHY: I don't know. You know. Your actions could not have been as bad as mine. I would not think. I don't know what they were.

ANN: You say mine could not have been as bad as yours.

CATHY: Many have, aggrandized this or that minor act, disloyalty, desertion, and thought these fantasies were . . .

ANN: . . . fantasies . . .

CATHY: Unforgivable. And scourged themselves. Like the nun with sexual thoughts. But fantasy is not sin.

ANN: . . . you . . .

CATHY: But I have actually sinned. And have been punished for it.

ANN: And does that cleanse you?

CATHY: The punishment? No.

ANN: What could cleanse you?

CATHY: Nothing but Christ.

(The phone rings.)

ANN *(Into the phone)*: Yes? No, I know they're here. *(Pause)* No. I'll tell you.

(She hangs up. Pause.)

CATHY: I'm sorry. That I am taking up so much of your time. And I thank you for your time.

ANN: You're quite welcome. *(Pause)* You said that Christ would cleanse you.

CATHY: Christ has cleansed me.

ANN: How?

CATHY: Truly?

ANN: Yes. How?

CATHY: Through His Blood, which means, through repentance.

ANN: With respect. How would one credit it?

CATHY: I did not ask you to credit it.

ANN: For, again with respect, one often hears the story . . .

CATHY: Yes, I understand . . .

ANN: Repeated here . . .

CATHY: I don't ask you to credit it.

ANN: But you brought it up.

CATHY: In answer to your question.

ANN: You wrote that you adore your Savior.

CATHY: You'd be within your right to doubt it.

ANN: Would I?

CATHY: As you say, it's a common ruse.

ANN: But I might credit it because of your book?

CATHY: You might.

ANN: What would impede me?

CATHY: If the book were written to impress. Or to delude. Or . . .

ANN: . . . yes?

CATHY: Or you might credit it because of my behavior. Because of my acts while here.

ANN: What if they were done to impress?

CATHY: What if the actions of Saints were done to impress? We don't know their motives. Or from delusion. The Prophets were demonstrably mad.

ANN: They were Mad?

CATHY: They'd seen *God*.

ANN: Have you seen God?

CATHY: I would like to see my father.

ANN: Have you seen God?

CATHY: Your question is if I am mad? . . . Because I found some understanding.

ANN: All right that . . . ?

CATHY: That however much we suffer. We could not suffer as completely as He.

ANN: As Jesus.

CATHY: Yes.

ANN: And is that "Finding God"?

CATHY: I don't know if it's finding God. But I know it's the meaning of The Christ. (*Pause*) I would like to see my father.

ANN: I know. He's unwell.

CATHY: He's dying.

ANN: Yes. It's been in the press.

CATHY: I would like to talk to him.

ANN: What would Mrs. Anderson say?

CATHY: Is that important?

ANN: What would she say?

CATHY: Is she here?

ANN: Of course.

CATHY: How is she?

ANN: What would she say to your request?

CATHY: We know what she'd say.

ANN: And is she incorrect?

(Pause.)

You say that you'd like to see your father.

CATHY: Yes.

ANN: After all this time.

CATHY: I'd like to talk with him.

ANN: About what?

CATHY: About God.

ANN: And would you bring him your manuscript?

CATHY: No.

ANN: Why?

CATHY: I believe it would upset him.

ANN: Why?

CATHY: My father's a Jew.

(Pause.)

ANN: Would he think it Heresy?

CATHY: Well, it might be, to his mind, just the one more crime.

ANN: To have changed your "covenant."

CATHY: That's right.

ANN: Is it a crime?

CATHY: No. People change.

ANN: And you want to talk to him about God.

CATHY: I want to . . . I want, no.

ANN: You said you want to talk to him about God.

CATHY: I want him to experience Grace.

ANN: Through Christ.

CATHY: No, he won't embrace Christ.

ANN: Then how would you enable him to Experience Grace? Believing as you do? (*Pause*) You're tired.

CATHY: Yes.

ANN (*Reads from a file*): You didn't have breakfast.

CATHY: They offered it to me.

ANN: Would you like me to get something . . . ?

(*She picks up the phone.*)

CATHY: I want to see my father. To allow him to Forgive me.

ANN (*Pause; puts the phone down*): Is it your intention to publish the book?

CATHY: If I were to be allowed. Or of course . . .

ANN: Yes?

CATHY: If I were released.

ANN: In which case . . . ?

CATHY: I would need no permission.

(*Pause.*)

ANN: The royalties . . .

CATHY: The royalties, would, under the law, still accrue to the Families. If I . . . if I *remained* . . .

ANN: And if you were released?

CATHY: After my father's death, I'm going to assign them the money.

ANN: The *royalties*?

CATHY: No. My inheritance.

ANN: You're going to give them part of your inheritance?

CATHY: No. All of it.

(*Pause.*)

ANN: That's an extraordinary sum of money.

CATHY: That's right.

DAVID MAMET

22

ANN: Does it concern you that the Board might consider that a sort of bribe.

CATHY: Perhaps it is.

ANN: And is it?

CATHY: My motives are sufficiently opaque to me. I doubt the Board can see them clearly.

ANN: I believe the Board might consider that a bribe.

CATHY: Then don't *tell* them. I'm not telling the Board. I'm telling you.

ANN: To influence my decision?

CATHY: Can you *conceive* of any *thing* that one in my position might do with a different motive? *(Pause)* I'm an old woman. I would like to be released.

ANN: I understand. Upon what grounds?

CATHY: Would you mock me for suggesting "kindness."

ANN: "Kindness to the wicked is cruelty to the Just." Where is that written?

CATHY: I don't know.

ANN: It's in the Bible. Isn't it?

CATHY: I . . .

ANN: It's in Proverbs.

CATHY: *I* don't know . . .

ANN *(Looking at files)*: But you studied The Bible. You're on record. As having requested a copy. A, a Bible. Some time ago. *(Reads)* "A Concordance Bible" . . . to replace . . .

CATHY: Yes. The other was lost.

ANN: To "continue your studies." It was . . .

CATHY: . . . yes.

ANN *(Checks file)*: "Lost, misplaced, or stolen." In your last move.

CATHY: Who would steal a religious book?

ANN: Someone might. With your notes. And your name in it.

CATHY: Why?

ANN: To sell it. *(Pause)* For quite a bit of money.

(Ann takes the Bible from her briefcase and hands it to Cathy.)

"A Concordance Bible."

CATHY: Yes. I remember it. At the beginning.

ANN: You may keep it.

CATHY: I remember it. Thank you.

ANN: You're welcome.

CATHY: How . . . ?

ANN: It was advertised. In a rare book catalog. And it was purchased.

CATHY: . . . yes?

ANN: For quite a lot of money. And it came to the notice of the Board.

CATHY: What happened to the money?

ANN: What do you think?

CATHY: It went to the Officer's family?

ANN: Eventually. That's correct.

(Pause.)

CATHY: Who stole it?

ANN: I am not permitted to "discuss a criminal enterprise" with you. Isn't it funny?

CATHY: And who bought it?

ANN: I . . .

CATHY: At the auction. Was it an auction?

ANN: Yes.

CATHY: Whoever bought it. His money. Was it returned to him?

ANN: No.

CATHY: Why?

ANN: As he was party to a crime.

CATHY: But perhaps he didn't know the book was stolen.

ANN: And perhaps he did.

CATHY: But that seems harsh.

ANN: In any case . . .

CATHY: If he didn't know the book was stolen, might the State return the money to him?

ANN: I don't know the law. Do you recall the Notations? *(Reads aloud)* "While the unafflicted may toy with an entertaining doubt, The Blind must believe the number of steps in the staircase Cannot Vary."

CATHY: Oh, my, and someone made a lot of money. Selling that.

ANN: Who are the unafflicted?

CATHY: I'm not sure.

ANN: Who are The Blind?

CATHY: I'm not sure that I wrote it.

ANN: But who could have written it?

CATHY: Someone who, who took it from me.

ANN: The "thief," someone who robs is called a "thief."

CATHY: Yes. They're called a thief. But it seems harsh. That some-one who may have purchased it in good faith should suffer.

ANN: I don't know the law.

CATHY: The officer's family are here?

ANN: That's right.

CATHY: I always assume that they are. How are they?

ANN: As you might expect.

CATHY: I always picture them. As they were then. As much as I know that they aren't. Do you know? I saw the newspa-pers. After one of our meetings. Eight or nine years ago? Showing my photo. From the time at the Apartment. And I thought, "Oh, poor defrauded reading public. Beautiful, young totem. What can have become of her?"

ANN: They let you read the Papers?

CATHY: Well, sometimes the rules need interpretation.

ANN: For?

CATHY: The new Guards. And the new Girls. To whom would they look for guidance?

ANN: And you guide them.

CATHY: If I can.

ANN: And do you Love them?

CATHY: Do I have sex with them?

ANN: Yes.

(*Pause.*)

CATHY: Do you know, I've always felt your thoughts were fixed in adolescence.

ANN: How so?

CATHY: On the Sin and Wonder of your body.

ANN: Is that adolescence?

CATHY: Oh yes. But the body grows old. And an appropriate notice of it would lead us to finish with Sin and to think on death. And what is beyond death.

ANN: What is beyond death?

CATHY: Christ. And the potential of redemption. No, of course I loved them. As they loved me. Why should they not? *That's* a question for you. Ann. But it begins to come back. Doesn't it? When one is being set free?

ANN: . . . it begins . . . ?

CATHY: When our possessions are few. And we review our thoughts.

ANN: And what do we find?

CATHY: Regret.

(Pause.)

ANN: What do I regret?

CATHY: Would you like to tell me?

ANN: Do I know?

CATHY: You said: "Was he your lover?" You said: "Did the women love you?" After all this time . . . *(Pause)* You could have had any woman here that you wanted.

ANN: It doesn't escape you that would have meant breaking my oath.

CATHY: None the less

ANN: Do I lack Sex?

CATHY: You lack *something*. Which is equal. In your mind. To the lack of sex. And, so, is signalized by it. And if you *name* it . . .

ANN: When did you take to psychiatry? . . .

CATHY: In Algeria, I was troubled. Guillaume asked me. And I said, "No, I don't *know* what's troubling me." He said, "If you *did*, what would it be?"

ANN: And so? . . .

CATHY: And so, Ann? So I told him.

ANN: Be? . . .

CATHY: Because I didn't want to be a coward.

ANN: . . . to be a coward.

CATHY: No. I knew I was a coward. But I wanted to be Brave.

ANN: And what was it that troubled you?

CATHY: What do you think?

ANN: If it were "conscience" why would overcoming it have been an act of courage?

(Pause.)

CATHY: Can people change?
ANN: I don't know.
CATHY: If they had changed, could you recognize it? *(Pause)* If there were any thing that I could do for you. I'd do it. *(Pause)* If it were *this close*. And you only had to ask for it. Because, that's what he had correct, do you see? *(Pause)* That it's always *close* . . . How do we know it is Redemption? Because it begins with Shame. That's true, Ann. That's what it means to pray. It means to confess. It's the worst pain. Our Savior Himself, Ann, needed help to bear the Cross.
ANN: I . . .
CATHY: But he *did* bear it, Ann. He did. Though terrified. And thought himself forsaken. Like you. *(Pause)* Like me.
ANN: I . . .

(Ann starts to speak. The phone rings. It rings again. Ann answers it.)

(Into the phone) Yes? No, presently. Please, please apologize to the . . . and make them comfortable. *(She hangs up)* Well.

(Pause.)

CATHY: Oh. *(Pause)* Then, are we done? . . .

(Ann checks her notes.)

ANN: Who are "the People"?
CATHY: Ann, you know who the people are.
ANN: Am I one of them?
CATHY: Say it was written by another woman.
ANN: The Speech?

CATHY: Yes.

ANN: And the other woman was you?

CATHY: A man killed and spent his life in anguish. And he asked Christ if He could forgive a man who had killed.

ANN: And Christ said?

CATHY: Christ said, "No. But you are now *another* man. For now in Me you are reborn."

ANN: Are you reborn?

CATHY: You find the concept arrogant. It's quite the opposite. It means *acceptance*.

ANN: Of?

CATHY: The human condition.

ANN: Are you the people?

CATHY: I am of the people.

ANN: And yet you come from great wealth.

CATHY: I renounced their wealth.

ANN: . . . and.

CATHY: I renounce it now . . .

ANN: And attended prestigious schools . . .

CATHY: And I renounced their teachings. And the *wealth* I renounce, my father's wealth, I . . .

ANN: . . . you . . .

CATHY: I understand. *You* might say, I'm going to work with the Sisters, and, so . . .

ANN: . . . you . . .

CATHY: And so will not *require* wealth . . .

ANN: . . . with the Sisters. *Why?*

CATHY: Because they will have me. (*Pause*) I wanted . . . to be cloistered.

ANN: . . . as you are here?

CATHY: But of my own choice. I fantasized that I could trade Shame for Degradation. And "wash the privies with my hair." To play the *piano* for them.

ANN: You said you had forgotten you studied the piano.

CATHY: . . . *and* equitation, *and* French. When I was young. When it was thought that it was a presumption. On the part of a Jew. (*Pause*) Listen: All evil regimes. Pressed their adherents into monstrous acts. As, afterwards, the actors could not face themselves, and so had to collude

DAVID MAMET

28

with the only society which could abide them. To *break* from those regimes, is, therefore, an act of wrenching. It is a sort of death. *(Pause)* I do not require wealth, and, so, the act of renunciation, you are correct, is perhaps, insufficient penance. But it is all I have.

(Pause.)

ANN: You do not require wealth.

CATHY: That's right.

ANN: As?

CATHY: As I'm going to work with the Sisters. I was going to say "in poverty," but I'm not sure I remember what that word means.

ANN: Why do you want to work with them?

CATHY: I've told you. Can I dissect myself and find a self-serving intention? Of course. But would it be more true than an altruistic one?

ANN: Which might be?

CATHY: That people are suffering. Should we not do what we can? To alleviate pain?

ANN: And the families of the Policemen.

CATHY: . . . yes?

ANN: We know that they suffer. Are they Of the People? Can they be? Or are the People specifically, but those whom you specify? All others being allowed to suffer?

CATHY: All people suffer.

ANN: Is that true?

CATHY: You suffer.

ANN: How do you know?

CATHY: Because I've watched you.

ANN: How do I suffer?

CATHY: I've told you.

ANN: Why do I suffer?

CATHY: The question is not what or why one suffers, but what recourse one may have.

ANN: And the answer is?

CATHY: Submission.

ANN: To?

CATHY: I've told you that, too.

ANN: Tell me again.

CATHY: Our Savior.

ANN: And where did you learn that?

CATHY: At the only place at which it may be learned. The Foot of the Cross.

ANN: Yes. But you were born a Jew. *(Pause)* "Christ was a Jew"?

CATHY: Christ *is* a Jew. And to mock the possibility of salvation is to mock Him. Whom you profess, by the cross around your neck, to worship. But you cannot worship Him, for to do so is to Renounce the Worship of your sorrows. Which is to say of yourself.

ANN: Is that so?

CATHY: And when you leave here; having, to your mind, wasted your life. On, what you understand as a fool's errand, you will, to your mind, have nothing. And you know it.

ANN: Was it a fool's errand?

CATHY: I believe you think it was.

ANN: But was it?

CATHY: You must say. If you are strong enough to say. I don't think that you are.

ANN: Why would that be?

CATHY: Which is why you toy with me.

ANN: How do I toy with you?

CATHY: You've moved my cell.

ANN: All right. Why have I moved your cell?

CATHY: For out-processing.

ANN: Which conclusion you arrive at? As?

CATHY: You're leaving. And want to conclude here with an Act of Grace. I understand.

(Pause.)

ANN: What did you plan to do on your release?

CATHY: I've told you.

ANN: To "Work with the Sisters." You . . .

CATHY: . . . you have that correspondence.

ANN: To "Work with the Sisters." Doing "Good."

CATHY: That's right.

ANN: And would you like to do Good.

CATHY: With all my heart.

ANN: Where is Althea?

(*Pause.*)

CATHY: Althea . . .

ANN: Yes.

CATHY: Why Althea? Finally?

ANN: Tell me.

CATHY: Is she the last one left?

ANN: Marty, of course, died in the apartment. Marianne died in the shoot-out . . . John and Jack . . .

CATHY: I know what happened to John and Jack.

ANN: Do they write you?

CATHY: No.

ANN: They don't?

CATHY: If they did I wouldn't accept their letters.

ANN: Oh, yes, as they were "traitors"? Were they traitors?

CATHY: If it amuses you, you may say that they were.

ANN: To what?

CATHY: All right.

ANN: To what?

CATHY: To "The Cause."

ANN: What was The Cause?

CATHY: There was no Cause.

ANN: But you've said that they were traitors.

CATHY: That's right.

ANN: But, to what, if not "The Cause"?

CATHY: . . . and they sinned.

ANN: Against what, if not "The Cause"?

CATHY: We all sin.

ANN: But can they have no forgiveness? You say you have found forgiveness. Can you not forgive them?

CATHY: Which of us is perfect?

ANN: You wrote that Althea was perfect.

CATHY: I wrote that?

ANN: At the beginning.

CATHY: You may read my letters if you like.

ANN: I may read them with or without your permission. They were found in the apartment.

CATHY: Ah, yes.

ANN: And, so, are in Evidence.

CATHY: Of course.

ANN: And, further, you, who believed in the "cleansing force of Violence," are powerless to stop me. As power comes, as you've said, "from the end of a gun."

CATHY: I have embraced Christ, and have renounced violence.

ANN: But you will not forgive "traitors."

CATHY: I said I have embraced Christ. Not that I have become Him.

(Pause.)

ANN: You believe. That the time has come. For us to release you. An old woman. Not that she deserves compassion. But that she no longer poses a threat. Is that the gist of your plea?

CATHY: Look at me.

ANN: All right

CATHY: Am I a threat?

ANN: Where is Althea?

CATHY: I don't know.

ANN: If you knew, would you tell me?

CATHY: What can that question mean? . . .

ANN: Who are The Blind?

CATHY: "The Blind . . ."

ANN *(Reads)*: "While the unafflicted may toy with the notion . . ."

CATHY: Yes, I wrote it. The, the . . .

ANN: Who are The Blind?

CATHY: I don't know.

ANN: But you wrote it. "The . . ."

CATHY: Yes, I wrote it, but people change. You change.

ANN: Who are "the unafflicted"?

CATHY: I . . .

ANN: Would that be you? What is the affliction you escaped?

CATHY: I . . .

ANN: Which allowed you such freedom? "Hov'ring at the margins of the real . . . We strive to disabuse ourselves . . ."

CATHY: They were the writings of a child. Who had the facility to ape that language. I confess. Now I have nothing more to confess.

ANN: Where is Althea?

CATHY: I don't know.

ANN: I don't believe you.

CATHY: What if you are wrong?

ANN: Then you must stay in prison.

CATHY: How is this diff . . .

ANN: Or whom . . .

CATHY: . . . how is this different from an inquisition?

ANN: Or whom would you have judge? And on what basis? That people may kill, as they are moved or inspired, and then claim they've had a "Vision." Of repentance? Of . . .

CATHY: Yes, all right.

ANN: Or simply claim "the biddability of childhood."

CATHY: I would like to go free.

ANN: Then tell me where your partner is.

CATHY: Is that the condition? Of my release?

ANN: John and Jack. Renounced their crime. By indicting their associate.

CATHY: Oh, yes, that's well put.

ANN: Which differs, you must agree, from, a mere "profession of faith" or of "repentance."

CATHY: Yes, you are correct. It does.

ANN: It was a quantifiable Act.

CATHY: All right.

ANN: Of which the Court took notice.

CATHY: Fine.

ANN: How else could it judge? By the ability of the claimants to awake "compassion"? Do you live in that sort of a world? Did you? You understand my problem. (Pause) You were lonely. After she left you.

CATHY: Yes. Let's do that, too.

ANN: You were lonely. When she "broke up with you."

CATHY: Yes.

ANN: When she "abandoned" you.

CATHY: If you will.

ANN: No, that's your word. Yes? In the letter you had passed to her?

CATHY: That was so long ago.

ANN: That you, illegally, had passed to her.

CATHY: I thought she had abandoned me.

ANN: You were imprisoned.

CATHY: Did you long for your children when you were apart from them? . . . *(Pause)* She ceased writing to me. And I pined for her.

ANN: Where is she?

CATHY: I don't know.

ANN: You don't know, and yet you wrote, last month, to your attorney: "I would like, in Freedom, to . . ."

CATHY: That letter was privileged.

ANN: "Once again . . ."

CATHY: That was a privileged communication.

ANN: "Gaze upon the Morning Star." And asked him . . .

CATHY: No, your interception . . .

ANN: To see if he could aid you in that.

CATHY: Your interception of that letter to my attorney is a crime.

ANN: Perhaps. If one believed in the State.

CATHY: Irrespective of . . .

ANN: "To gaze," you wrote, "again upon the Morning Star." What is the Morning Star?

(Pause.)

CATHY: The Morning Star is Venus.

ANN: In this context.

CATHY: It was the star of Bethlehem and—as the Star of Evening—shone into the cave where Christ was born.

ANN: In this context.

CATHY: That's what it means.

ANN: Yes. But the phrase also occurs here. In your Concordance Bible, in the Book of Esther. Where, in the margin, we find: "Esther, who is also Astarte and Ishtar. Whence our word star." And a poem. "Written in sequestration. To Althea. I long . . ."

CATHY: All right . . .

ANN: "To gaze, once again. Upon you: on the Morning Star." Where is Althea?

CATHY: You, understandably, assume, that that which is . . .

ANN: "Withheld"?

CATHY: You assume. That everything that's said here, which is, of necessity, *opaque* . . .

ANN: . . . why would it be "*opaque*"?

CATHY: Must, of necessity, be criminal, or shameful. That it must be *sexual*, or . . .

ANN: Is love between two women shameful?

CATHY: It's *private*. Do you understand? As sex between any two people is private. The unhealthy may confuse the wish for privacy with shame. Do you want me to tell you my *fantasies*? To . . .

ANN: Everything said here is said in confidence.

CATHY: Oh, please. You inform the Board . . .

ANN: All I forward to the Board are my *conclusions*.

CATHY: How are they arrived at? If prurience . . .

ANN: . . . am I prurient? . . .

CATHY: . . . and curiosity are confused? If a desire for *privacy* is confused with . . .

ANN: I . . .

CATHY: One lies, wait, or, say one *withholds* . . .

ANN: Everyone who sits there lies, I understand. I would.

CATHY: You would . . .

ANN: To go free, yes, of course.

CATHY: And yet, and yet—*knowing* that, you indulge, in the name of, what? "Psychology," your penchant for what, "observation"?

ANN: Is love between women unnatural?

CATHY: Everything in prison is unnatural. Would you like me to set you free?

ANN: How would you set me free?

CATHY: No. Would you *like* me. To set you free?

ANN: How am I bound?

CATHY: Will you answer me?

ANN: You wrote: "The troubled cannot be freed by psychiatry." That they do not *lack* psychiatry.

CATHY: . . . that's right.

ANN: ". . . they lack love." (*Pause*) Do I lack love?

CATHY: Of course you do.

ANN: . . . I lack love . . .

CATHY: That's why you're *frightened*.

ANN: I'm frightened. Why?

CATHY: Because you're leaving.

ANN: Has my work here given me Love?

CATHY: It's given you *structure*. Which is to say, *repression* . . .

ANN: *Sexual* repression?

CATHY: Of a deeper desire.

ANN: For?

CATHY: Submission.

ANN: To?

CATHY: To God. (*Pause*) Which is why you mock the possibility in others. I understand. Believe me.

(*Pause.*)

ANN: Where is Althea?

CATHY: *Put it down.* Don't you see? You are chained to the past. When you can be free. This is the lesson of The Christ. To let the dead bury the dead. That is all that it means, Ann, to be reborn. It is not "mystical" that you need be frightened of it. It is not an "ordeal" it is a *gift*. The end of regret. It's faith. It is the holy ghost.

ANN: What is the Holy Ghost?

CATHY: It is that Spirit which unites the Father and the Son. It is a mystery. Which is the essence of Faith. Ann: Neither God nor human worth can be proved. That, finally, there is nothing but Spirit. In time. I could by Reason, Ann, bring you to Faith. I know your heart is heavy.

ANN: Why is my heart heavy?

CATHY: Because it is stone. Which must break to be opened. Will you break open your heart? You can lay your burden down. And He will *take* it from you.

(*The phone rings again.*)

I can't do it for you, Ann. I wish I could. He can.

(*The phone rings again.*)

But it requires an act of courage.

(*Ann picks up the phone and holds it.*)

ANN: Where is Althea?
CATHY: Are you *sure*? Are you *sure*?
ANN: I . . .
CATHY: If I can *help* you. I'll *help* you. Why would I not? You *know* I've helped others. You *know* I have.

(*Ann picks up the phone.*)

ANN (*Into the phone*): Thank you. I understand.
CATHY: . . . what do you think that I've been *doing* here? . . . Is it impossible that I was sent here? Or, finding myself here found that I might do good, might that not be called the intercession of God? Whose only worldly influence, Ann, is through the human soul. Which is to say, through sinners. "There was a young girl who killed. And was confined to prison. And a man gave her a book."
ANN: Where is Althea?
CATHY: I don't know.
ANN: But you wrote to her.
CATHY: I wrote *of* her.
ANN: Oh yes. (*Reading*) "I thought she was dead. And searched for her. In other women . . ."
CATHY: . . . all right . . .
ANN (*Reading*): "Assured that their outward form was but a necessary veil. To keep the mystery from profane eyes. A common reaction, I learned, of the widow."
CATHY: For all I know, she is dead. For all I know, she is somewhere in Custody.
ANN: And someone has been holding her? All of these years.
CATHY: You say it doesn't happen? . . .
ANN: Does it?

CATHY: That the State . . .

ANN: Are you an Enemy of the State?

CATHY: I was.

ANN: And now? Are you an Enemy of the State?

CATHY: No.

ANN: But you were.

CATHY: Yes.

ANN: What are the ways in which enemies may be reconciled?

CATHY: . . . all right . . .

ANN (*Reads*): "These are the ways in which Enemies can be reconciled."

CATHY: I was young. And I was a fool.

ANN: "Surrender of life, of property, of land, or of Prejudice," which I understand to mean, of a previously held belief.

CATHY: Have you done nothing, in your youth . . .

ANN: "Or, in plainer English, Enemies may be reconciled if one or both recant, revise or surrender their position." Which do we find here?

CATHY: I don't know.

ANN: How can I know unless you tell me?

CATHY: Do you enjoy my discomfort?

ANN: You chose to come here. To see me.

CATHY: That's right.

ANN: Seeking approval for your request. Which request may only be obtained through my endorsement.

CATHY: Which may only be obtained from *you*.

ANN: That's right.

(*Pause.*)

CATHY: All right, "why?"

ANN: Because I have been delegated that power.

CATHY: And why *you*?

ANN: As a representative of the State.

CATHY: "With all your imperfections."

ANN: Did you assume: your request, might be effected without, at the *least* some discomfort? I will not say anger, shame or hatred on your part? Did you assume I would not probe you.

CATHY: Delegating *power* . . .

ANN: Oh, yes. As we find, in your book . . . May be understood as *cowardice*, both on the part . . .

CATHY: . . . delegating power . . .

ANN: . . . in your *letters*. No. I beg your pardon. In your *talks*. In your *pamphlet* . . . in . . .

CATHY: And they're hardly "talks," and, "delegating power," yes, *must* imply superior, superior . . .

ANN: . . . but wasn't that the essence of your Movement? Teaching the ignorant that "they have the power."

CATHY: The power wasn't ours to give. It was theirs.

ANN: And you were simply "reminding" them.

CATHY: We . . .

ANN: Is that what you were doing?

CATHY: We thought we were "awakening" them.

ANN: How had you been awakened?

CATHY: I hadn't been awakened. *Now* I . . .

ANN: Yes. But I'm asking you now. What did you think then? How could you wake them, if you, if . . .

CATHY: My political views of that time . . .

ANN: By what superiority on your part? Do you see?

CATHY: . . . ah-hah . . .

ANN: . . . had you been granted that revelation?

CATHY: My political views, of that time.

(*Pause.*)

ANN: Go on . . .

CATHY: Having been convicted, and those views offered in . . .

ANN: "Illegally"?

CATHY: . . . whether illegally or not, in support of my guilt, they, after my conviction, must become moot.

ANN: Yes?

CATHY: According to the Law.

ANN: All right.

CATHY: And you debarred from interrogating me concerning them.

ANN: All right.

CATHY: No, it's not all right. Or am I meant to be perpetually persecuted . . .

ANN: But . . .

CATHY: No. No. What does it mean? That someone has "said" this or that? Or "mouthed a doctrine"? It's words. It's sounds. It changes nothing.

ANN: It's mere words.

CATHY: That's right.

ANN: But you acted upon them.

CATHY: That's not what I was tried for. Unless it was a political crime. Was it a political crime?

ANN: . . . I.

CATHY: No, if my "views" could not be adduced in mitigation of my crime they cannot be adduced *now* to extend my . . .

ANN: I . . .

CATHY: . . . to extend my punishment. Separate the speech, which you declare was mere foolishness.

ANN: . . . except . . .

CATHY: . . . and I *agree* with you.

ANN: . . . except . . .

CATHY: No. There is the *pamphlet*. And there is the *crime*. If they are *linked*, then I am being persecuted. If I am only being punished for the crime *with which I was charged*. I have served my term. I beg your pardon. You were speaking.

(*Pause.*)

ANN: When you *taught*. In Algeria, all right . . .

CATHY: No. It's *not* all right. Who, God knows, has paid for her actions.

ANN: When you, at the Farm, at the Apartment, "strove to awaken" the Masses . . .

CATHY: They lived, as many do, contentedly, in ignorance of their state. As many do today. As *you* do. In their relationship to the Divine. We live in ignorance.

ANN: But you did not live in ignorance.

CATHY: We felt that we did not.

ANN: Then how had you been elevated? Do you see? As, you say, *again*, you have been?

CATHY: I have been raised by Christ.

ANN: Yes. But they . . . If they lived in contentment. Then . . .

CATHY: If they "lived in contentment"? They were *oppressed*.

ANN: But what raised you? To that understanding? A Book? A Man? *(She reads)* "A moment of enlightenment, the religious would say the experience of Grace."

CATHY: I was not writing about the Man.

ANN: No, you were writing about Christ. But: the language you used, in your "talks," it's the same *language* . . . "Hov'ring at the margins of the real . . ."

CATHY: You don't have to demean them, by calling them "talks."

ANN: What are they, "Speeches"?

CATHY: But they're hardly "talks."

ANN: What are they?

CATHY: Interactions. Or, "Thoughts," perhaps, "Meditations" . . .

ANN: Well, yes, but you see, the inability to call things by their names, may lead, in you and in your, what did you say? "Revolution"? No less than in the State, to imprecision. And, in our case, certainty has led to error. Or, did you act in Error? Did you act in Error?

CATHY: When?

(Pause.)

ANN: What is "murder"?

CATHY: It is the unlawful taking of a human life.

ANN: Indeed it is. Did you commit murder?

CATHY: I was adjudged guilty of murder.

ANN: Did you commit murder?

CATHY: I have worked. For thirty-five years, to discharge. My "debt to society."

ANN: Which Society still sticks upon the one point. What is that point? And why should I believe that you might be a "member of society," if you are incapable even of a half-hour's courteous interaction with me in this room? A person from whom you desire a great service—and yet you are incapable of stilling your rage.

CATHY: That's not true . . .

ANN: . . . that you should be reduced . . .

CATHY: . . . it's simply not true.

ANN: To comply with a requirement of the State. That you divulge the whereabouts of your accomplice. Who killed alongside you. Which legitimate, which is to say "lawful" demand, you characterize as an "inquisition" . . .

CATHY: . . . my father is dying. Should . . .

ANN: . . . I'm sorry.

CATHY: . . . should a person. Not be left. A sense . . . finally . . .

ANN: . . . go on.

(Pause.)

CATHY: A sense of dignity.

(Pause.)

ANN: I have no doubt that you consider yourself, I will not insult you by using the term "rehabilitated" . . .

CATHY: I don't know that I know the meaning of the word.

ANN: It means "re-clothed"—its implication being "restored."

CATHY: No doubt. But how may one be restored who is, in the eyes of the State, bound or free, always a criminal?

ANN: "How can the criminal not see that the same sense of entitlement which led him to crime leads him to demand a societal amnesia regarding his conviction." Who wrote that?

CATHY: You surprise me.

ANN: Who wrote it?

CATHY: Lombroso.

ANN: And at what conclusion did he arrive, after a lifetime of his studies?

CATHY: You impress me.

ANN: At what conclusion did he arrive?

CATHY: That there is no solution to the problem of Crime.

ANN: Except?

CATHY: Deterrence, punishment, and incarceration.

ANN: And what did he say about "Rehabilitation"?

CATHY: You impress me, Ann.

ANN: Yes, you said. "That Criminology . . ."

CATHY: "Criminology, as any study claiming the imprimatur of science, must rest upon observation, but that all observation in prison is corrupt."

ANN: Go on.

CATHY: "For there all function under unnatural restraint, and one can no more usefully reason from measurements made there than from that of wild animals caged in a zoo."

ANN: What is September 25th?

CATHY: It is the anniversary of the Robbery.

ANN: How might others understand it?

CATHY: Who?

ANN: We have very little time.

CATHY: It is the anniversary of the death of the two officers.

ANN: And who might understand it as such?

CATHY: Their families.

ANN: Their *families*. Have . . .

CATHY: I know . . .

ANN: For thirty-five years.

CATHY: I know they have.

ANN: Sat. On these occasions . . . In that anteroom . . .

CATHY: What do you want?

ANN: While I, and while my predecessor . . .

CATHY: Yes. The "Families . . ."

ANN: And Mrs. Fiske, who is . . .

CATHY: I know who she is.

ANN: Who is she?

CATHY: Officer Shay's . . .

ANN: Yes. Do you see? Officer Shay's daughter. Which became the definition of her life. She could not attend. Her son could not attend, as he is caring for his mother, who is ill. And they write to say what? What is their request?

CATHY: Call the guard.

ANN: To ask . . . what?

CATHY: Call the guard.

ANN: To plead, in the name of justice. That you be left to die in Prison. *(Pause)* *My* task. Is to overcome my feelings.

And attempt to rule, if I can, impartially, upon the case. I understand your feelings . . .

CATHY: Is that so?

ANN: . . . and in spite of them, and mine, attempt to employ, yes, I think I . . .

CATHY: What are they?

ANN: My feelings?

CATHY: Yes, what are . . . ?

ANN: Is it beyond you that one might succeed in keeping them in check? And that it's *laudable*? Is there a *name* for this?

CATHY: All right.

ANN: Is it called "reserve"? Or "circumspection," or . . .

CATHY: . . . all right.

ANN: Might it be called restraint? (*Pause*) You would like to go free.

CATHY: Everyone here would like to go free.

ANN: Feeling that you have served more than a sufficiency of what you see as a cruel sentence . . .

CATHY: Do you think that it was cruel?

ANN: I understand the mentality of the judge who imposed it.

CATHY: Do you think it was cruel?

ANN: . . . I would like to think it was imposed in sorrow. I believe your crime frightened him, and that he acted to protect those he had sworn to protect.

CATHY: Was the sentence cruel?

ANN: It was cruel to *you*.

CATHY: And can you act to end the cruelty? Or would that be to rely upon your feelings? In this case "kindness."

ANN: It is an awesome power I have. Yes: It "comes from the end of a gun." As did yours. When you killed those officers. And I assure you, I know I, no less than you, will be held to account.

CATHY: Do you mean we all shall be held to account in Heaven? (*Pause*) Does not such a view, legally, unfit you to judge me?

ANN: How would that be?

CATHY: To invoke a system which . . .

ANN: "Religion"?

CATHY: . . . which . . .

ANN: . . . but *you* invoked religion . . .

CATHY: . . . a system which, I beg your pardon . . .

ANN: I judge to the best of my ability. According to the Law. It is not my personal theology, nor bias, nor, indeed "knowledge of Human Nature" which *permit* me to judge, but a dedication to the Law which *obligates* me. To do so.

(*Pause.*)

CATHY: And how is Mrs. Fiske.

ANN: She is unwell.

CATHY: Is she seriously ill?

ANN: She has dedicated her life to your punishment. I would assume she is. (*Pause*) You cried. When your friend abandoned you. And wrote to plead with her to "stay with you." And wrote your parents. With the first terms of affection. Since you were a child. Asking for comfort. As you had been harmed. Now you want to go free. And appeal, as does a child, to those in power. Seeking out power.

CATHY: What do you say about me?

ANN: Say about you . . .

CATHY: Yes, when . . .

ANN: I don't speak about you.

CATHY: At a dinner party, to a *friend* . . . if someone asks you. They must ask you.

ANN: Very little anymore.

CATHY: Oh.

ANN: Yes—you were famous once.

CATHY: All right. At the end of the day. Can you not overcome your animosity? . . .

ANN: As you have, Cathy? (*Pause*) Officer Shay. Had he lived he would have been what?

CATHY: Had he lived he would have been eighty-one.

ANN: Is that an old man?

CATHY: Is it an old man?

ANN: You want to live . . .

CATHY: Yes. I do. I assume all people do.

ANN: There was a time you didn't care to.

(*Pause.*)

CATHY: That's right.

ANN: Do you remember that?

CATHY: Yes.

ANN: You came to us then with a different request.

CATHY: Well. It's a long life.

ANN: And the longer we live the more we see things change. And bring us back to the beginning.

CATHY: And people cannot change?

ANN: I've yet to see it.

CATHY: But can you *imagine* it?

ANN: I think I can.

CATHY: In what would it consist? In your imagination. How would it be established? By a record such as mine, of service and of study? . . . or else, what are you *doing* here? If you cannot conceive an instance. Where your work could help? What do you want of me?

ANN: What do you think?

CATHY: I think you want revenge.

ANN: You feel subjecting you periodically to my questioning constitutes revenge?

CATHY: Do you know. What it's like. To *vacillate*. Between the desire to *please*. To, to embellish in order to please; or to be reticent, and fear your reserve will be misinterpreted as *sullenness*? When your freedom is at stake? Your very *freedom*?

ANN: Well, you broke the law. Didn't you. And you wanted to die. As once you were "thwarted in love." Poor thing. And counted yourself privileged. By your grievance. As you were imprisoned. And your lover abandoned you. She "left" you, and . . .

CATHY: . . . all right.

ANN: You wanted to die. As if she could "be" with you. In prison, what, "in death"? And dramatized yourself. As if no woman ever suffered in love. (*Studies papers*) You wrote. About her face: "Dreaming of her face." About the power of dreams: "What is the power of dreams? They have the power to release us . . . each morning." Period. "It's a new vision." Period. "Of a previously unsuspected depth of sorrow." (*Pause*) Many were moved. (*Pause*) Some thought you should have been allowed to die. When you wanted to die. And some prayed for your soul.

(Pause.)

Why did they pray for you?

CATHY: Because I was in pain.

ANN: No. They prayed for you as you expressed yourself well.

CATHY: Can you not control your hatred?

ANN: . . . as you have done in your book. "The love of Christ washes over me. And the sweet balm of forgiven . . ." You congratulate yourself for Christ's forgiveness. But you forgive no one. Do you? John and Jack? . . .

(Cathy rises.)

CATHY: Call the guard.

ANN: Sit down. I said: sit down. I'll see you in punitive detention do you hear me? For how long? Indefinitely. Which means forever. For Nobody Cares. Cathy. Your family has left you, your lover abandoned you, the officers' families live to desire your death, the public no longer remembers your name, and no one cares.

CATHY: Why do *you* care?

ANN: Because it's my duty.

CATHY: I think you are a voyeur.

ANN: Do you?

CATHY: I think you are a frustrated old woman, who gains enjoyment from her "charade of Probity."

ANN: . . . yes, I read that article.

CATHY: . . . that you are jealous.

ANN: Of?

CATHY: My life. Which you enjoy as a romance.

ANN: Of your life.

CATHY: Of loving *women* . . . of . . .

ANN: Of "violence"?

CATHY: Yes, of course, of violence.

ANN: Of sex and violence?

CATHY: Absolutely.

ANN: Are they related? Or are they only linked in your sickness?

CATHY: And what sickness is that?

ANN: You . . .

CATHY: I have surpassed them.

ANN: Have you?

CATHY: Why do you care?

ANN: Because I represent the State.

CATHY: The "State."

ANN: Yes. Without which who can make consequences equal? Who shall rebuke the evildoer, who comfort the luckless, except the State. Whose existence you decry.

CATHY: I . . .

ANN: First in your "Movement," then in "Christ." How are the two, then, not equal? Tell me that. (*Pause*) Every society has punished the murderer. If not, what meaning of "society"? But ours, you feel, should not. As you have "suffered enough." FOR WHOM? For yourself? Indeed, for who would embrace suffering? For the State? No. For the State confines you not to cause your suffering, but to ensure freedom to others.

CATHY: As I might kill again?

ANN: So that all will consider their acts and regard their consequence. And control themselves. Why do you plead to be excused? For the same reason you considered yourself free to kill. As you are "better"—you know better. You are entitled to "explore" the higher realms of behavior. To savor this or that thrill. And call it Theater of the Real. Theater of the Street. Violence as Cleansing . . . I read the pamphlets. I read that filth.

CATHY: They were the Folly of Youth.

ANN: They were not the Folly of Youth. They were evil, wicked heresy.

CATHY: What do you want of me?

ANN: Renounce them.

CATHY: I have renounced them. In my embrace of Christ.

ANN: I don't believe you.

CATHY: How could I make you believe me? Would you like me to beg.

ANN: You made the policeman beg. And then you shot him.

CATHY: Would you like me to beg.

ANN: I would like you to see.

CATHY: To see *what*?

ANN: That you, *systematically*, deny . . . that throughout your life . . . your "revelations" . . . *(Pause)* I would like you to accept your responsibility.

CATHY: Why?

ANN: Because I represent the State. And that's my duty.

CATHY: How would you *know*? That I had accepted . . .

ANN: . . . I . . .

CATHY: No. What? What would signal my conversion to you if not my acts here?

ANN: I . . .

CATHY: Tell me what you want. What you want. Finally.

(Pause.)

ANN: I want to save you.

CATHY: Why?

ANN: Because you have a soul.

CATHY: How do you know?

ANN: Because I have a soul.

(Pause.)

CATHY: Those who have served. *(Pause)* A Life term. Those who have . . .

ANN: Killed.

CATHY: I have no problem with the word. And have served, a term, of *thirty-five* years . . .

ANN: Your sentence is indeterminate.

CATHY: . . . may be released.

ANN: Because?

CATHY: Through lack of opposition. By the State allowing the usual definitions of the Indeterminate Sentence. Through judicial lethargy, or *sloth*, indeed, through chance or mischance . . .

ANN: But . . .

CATHY: But *finally*, if that release seems to the State the path least likely to bring upon itself additional work, anxiety, or trauma.

ANN: Yes. That's right. And my question to you is: How could it be otherwise? Unless you were "the special case"; and why would that be.

CATHY: I thought . . .

ANN: Yes?

CATHY: I thought that this meeting would be different.

ANN: Why?

CATHY: Because it was the end.

ANN: You thought it was the end because?

CATHY: Because you're leaving.

ANN: Well. Then it would be the end for me.

CATHY: Why are you toying with me? Your replacement, *must* endorse my parole. Based upon my behavior. Based upon Time Served . . . *far* . . .

ANN: But the Courts have denied . . .

CATHY: Far in excess, of that served for any similar crime.

ANN: We have discretion.

CATHY: Which, a new, nonprejudiced, *impartial* official must see, which so prolonged incarceration they must see as "cruel and unusual punishment."

ANN *(Simultaneous with "punishment")*: The Courts have ruled . . .

CATHY: *Much* of it, of course, at the, the, the instigation of: The Andersons, of Mrs. Fiske, of the *Policeman's* Union of . . .

ANN: And are they not entitled, to protest, to . . .

CATHY: They're *gone*. Those who were affected. The Policemen, the . . . They're *gone*.

ANN: Mrs. Anderson is not gone. Mrs. Fiske is not gone . . .

CATHY: . . . and a persistence, in my, contrary to all precedent . . .

ANN: Do you believe in Justice?

CATHY: . . . and the Court's refusal to hear. My latest appeals . . .

ANN: Do you deny the rights of the Andersons, or of the Police Union, to protest? . . .

CATHY: I beg your pardon. I . . .

ANN: No. You "protested" *didn't* you? With *violence*. With . . .

CATHY: I . . .

ANN: And called it "protest" although it was *crime*. And the courts have ruled, you are involved in an "ongoing criminal conspiracy." Which crime *has* no Statute of Limitations, which . . .

CATHY: "An ongoing . . ."

ANN: You communicated with your . . .

CATHY: . . . please

ANN: . . . criminal partner, a fugitive from just . . .

CATHY: And so you've given me *thirty-five years*. For, for, essentially, refusing to . . .

ANN: You might have left after the initial, minimum . . .

CATHY: For refusing to *inform*. I have repented my crime. I have served that sentence *four times* in excess of that which you would have imposed on a "mere" criminal. I am an Old Woman. I have done wrong. I have spoken my mind. My father is dying. It's time to let me go.

(The phone rings.)

ANN *(Into the phone)*: Yes. Yes. I know she's tired. Yes. I know. I'm finishing here. And then I'll come out. All right. Go ahead. *(She hangs up)*

CATHY: Mrs. Anderson.

ANN: That's right.

CATHY: She stayed, as usual, to hear . . .

ANN: Yes.

CATHY: And what will she do? When you tell her.

ANN: When I tell her what?

CATHY: Of my release. I beg your pardon. You haven't informed me of your decision.

ANN: No, that's right.

CATHY: But you've decided to release me.

ANN: Which you say because?

CATHY: You've changed my cell. For out-processing. *(Pause)* I've served my time. In Justice. As you know. You know that. *(Pause)* You say you would like to save me. And I thank you for the thought. Truly. As one who has found that which unites us. Which is the spirit of God. Which is the soul. I am imperfect. I am headstrong. I am arrogant. I am endeavoring to cleanse myself. In accepting that solace offered to me. The Sacrifice of Christ.

ANN: Oh, please. It's a lie.

CATHY: Is it my Resurrection you doubt, or the Existence of God?

ANN: Do you think I've worked here all these years and have learned nothing.

CATHY: For, don't you see? The two are the same.

ANN: It's a ruse, Cathy.

CATHY: Is it impossible I have found God? We read that Sinners found God. Do you deny it, Ann? It's in the Bible. Do you think I don't know what *you* suffer? It's called "doubt." It is the bar on the gateway to Belief. Christ doubted Himself, Ann, in Gethsemane. He doubted God. *Christ*, Ann. How can you believe that which you disbelieve? The Prayer must come *first*, Ann. "Lord Jesus, I have Sinned . . ." Is it not possible. If Christ rose from the dead, Ann, that he saved me? Even me—that I was *sent* here—to remind you. (*Pause*) Pray with me, Ann. "Lord Jesus, I have Sinned . . ."

ANN: Do you think I haven't prayed? For you, for the others, for Myself?

CATHY: Have you?	ANN: Do you think. It was less apparent to me, than to you, that I should question the worth of my "work" here?

CATHY: What did you pray for?

ANN: Do you think I'm *blind*?

CATHY: What did you pray for?

ANN (*Simultaneous with "pray"*): I prayed for forgiveness.

(*Pause.*)

CATHY: And did you find forgiveness? (*Pause*) Then the time has come to stop praying for, and to pray *to* God.

ANN: . . . in the midst of all this suffering . . .

CATHY: And pray *to* God.

ANN: . . . for one sign

CATHY: How would that sign appear, Ann? Could it be: the plea of a murderess? That you accept Christ. He told us, Ann, the heart is Stone. To open it must shatter.

ANN: I . . .

CATHY: It's called "doubt."

ANN: I . . .

CATHY: Open your Heart and be Saved.

(Pause.)

Lord. *(Pause)* Who ordains all things. Who took the most depraved of women and bid her to Your side to be the Queen of Heaven. Who blessed the good Thief with the vow that he would that day abide with Him. Thank you. For your miraculous gift of Grace. To this poor, wretched sinner. Thank you, Jesus. For permitting me to pray.

(Pause.)

ANN: Cathy, it's a lie.

CATHY: No.

ANN: It's a lie.

CATHY: Then Christ is a lie. You say you asked for a sign.

ANN: Yes.

CATHY: Of?

ANN: Redemption.

CATHY: It's here before you.

ANN: No.

CATHY: Then tell me what a sign would be.

ANN: If you revealed the location of your accomplice.

CATHY: No, I don't know it.

ANN: Cathy.

CATHY: Yes.

ANN: I know it's a lie.

CATHY: No. You *suspect* it's a lie. I'm asking you to trade suspicion for Faith.

ANN: Where is Althea?

CATHY: I don't know.

ANN: You asked what a sign would be. That your heart has changed.

CATHY: I cannot confess to that of which I have no knowledge. Even to save *you*.

ANN: If your heart has changed.

CATHY: My heart *has* changed.

ANN: Then . . .

CATHY: But how can I confess to that of which I'm ignorant? How . . . how . . .

ANN: Only in this room.

CATHY: The ultimate Corruption of Power is the belief that it can do all things. But with all its power the State cannot compel me to confess that which I do not know. The State . . .

ANN: Not the State, I swear to you . . .

CATHY: The State does not have the power.

ANN: . . . Just you and me. For me.

CATHY: . . . Neither to suspend the natural laws, nor to force me . . .

ANN: Cathy.

CATHY: To corrupt my . . .

ANN: Only in this room.

CATHY: They pleaded with Jesus: "Come down from the Cross. If you are the Christ."

ANN: Is it absurd to ask for a sign? . . .

CATHY: The sign was not that he descended the Cross, Ann, but that he did not. That is the meaning of Faith.

ANN: Not to go free?

(*Pause.*)

CATHY: You disappoint me. "Confess and Go Free." How does this differ from an Inquisition, which the laws, in their wisdom . . .

ANN: . . . Cathy

CATHY: No. The State does not have that power. To put me on the *Cross*? To . . .

ANN: *I* have that power. Do you understand? *I* have to choose. And you are in my power. As was the Officer, when you shot him to death.

CATHY *(To self)*: . . . oh.

ANN *(Reads)*: "Cathy shot the guard. Althea stood over the second officer, and shouted, 'he's a witness.' He crawled on his side, away from her, and Cathy shot him."

CATHY: No. You. Have put yourself into a false position. *(Pause)* You are a truthful woman. You've asked me to "*confess*," to establish, my suitability for release. But you know that is against the law. It is a criminal misuse of power.

ANN: I asked for a sign.

CATHY: And if not, *what*? Am I a witch? Do you think I'm the *devil*? Do you want to end your time here in *absurdity*? But then, it was all absurd, was it not? Your "Good Works" and your "Life of Sacrifice." And what has it brought you? Your child abandoned you, your husband left you. You have grown old. I have love waiting for me. You leave here with nothing. Having, you are correct, *accomplished* nothing. Which of the "clients" you've seen, over the years, has done anything but lie to you—while you took notes?? And you would lie, too. If the machine, which you serve, had oppressed, rather than co-opted you. You served a corrupt State in a failed institution. That's the story of your life . . . *Why*?

ANN: . . . all right.

CATHY: For the sick thrill of hearing women cry. And lie to you. To see them wonder, "Can I seduce her?" And you, who could have had *any* of them. Yes, as I did, had and have *nothing*. Having had nothing but *power*, and too weak to use it, and now it's gone. It's *you* who should confess. And then you would be saved. Give me a cigarette.

ANN: I haven't smoked for years.

CATHY: Does the girl have one?

ANN: I don't know.

CATHY: And shall I tell you what I plan to do?

ANN: When?

CATHY: I beg your pardon. No. You haven't "said" it.

ANN: But I've changed your cell. For "out-processing."

CATHY: Isn't it true?

ANN: No. (*Pause*) I've moved your cell. And have removed: your book. Your manuscript, and all of your drafts and notes. I want the location of your accomplice. And unless you give it to me, I'm going to burn the lot.

(*Pause.*)

CATHY: Do you fear me that much?

ANN: Yes, I do.

CATHY: Why?

ANN: Because you killed.

CATHY: Your successor will set me free. That's she, isn't it? In the outer office.

ANN: She will set you free because?

CATHY: Because she's *young*, because she's new, because she's stupid. And believes in the perfectibility of man. Against all evidence. She will read my book, and be moved by it. As will anyone. Who reads it.

ANN: Because?

CATHY: Because it reassures the frightened their passivity will keep them safe.

ANN: You didn't hear me. I'm going to have it destroyed.

CATHY: I. Will. Walk. Out of this office. Right now. Into hers. And tell her of your threat. And file a *complaint*, against you. Which must be heard; and the State will be debarred by law, from destruction of my property. In *fact*. They will be forced to review it—which is to say *read* it. And will be "moved" by it. Don't you see. All of your notions. All come down. To the willingness. Or the refusal to use force.

ANN: In service of "Historical Necessity"?

CATHY: Marx was a fool. And he was a Jew: No less a parasite than those he indicted, "writing."

ANN: Words have no power?

CATHY: "only to misdirect . . ."

ANN: As in your book.

CATHY: " . . . by what universal test do we know power?"

ANN: It comes from a gun?

CATHY: How else have you held me here? Through "natural right"? Through "a consensus of the governed"? People with guns were *paid* to keep me here. As someone Feared me.

ANN: . . . they feared your ideas.

CATHY: Ideas more vicious and violent than mine are entertained every day, in the minds of the most peaceful people on Earth. Doctrines more seditious are taught in the schools. They feared *me*.

ANN: As they should.

CATHY: That's right. And I'll tell you about your Brave Announcement. That you were interested in our sex.

ANN: Between Althea and you . . .

CATHY: People are seduced by the forbidden. The Weak? Are not "terrified" by this or that act of transgression—they're *thrilled* by it.

ANN: . . . thrilled by it? . . .

CATHY: What else is a newspaper? (*Pause*) People are killed every day . . .

ANN: And what are The Weak frightened by?

CATHY: The dissolution of their country.

ANN: "The country is dying"?

CATHY: "Dying bankrupt, and the wastrel children squabbling about the will."

ANN: He wrote well.

CATHY: It's nothing to write well.

ANN: "He fought well"?

CATHY: He fought, just as *you* fight. With the weapons at hand. With your guns.

ANN: Our guns are used to enforce . . .

CATHY: Laws made by whores, thugs and thieves who bribed their way to office. How many times must you see it?

ANN: What replaces it?

CATHY: It's long been replaced. (*Pause*) We were looting an empty house.

ANN: The Officer was there.

CATHY: Yes, that's too bad.

ANN: And you shot him.

CATHY: He was carrying a gun. He would have done better to use it.

(Ann walks to the conference table and presses a switch on the intercom.)

ANN *(Into the intercom)*: Did you hear that? Have it transcribed. I'll come out now to see Mrs. Anderson.

(She hangs up.)

CATHY: You have just sentenced me to a life in prison.
ANN: Yes?
CATHY: For speaking my mind.
ANN: Is that what I did?

(Pause.)

CATHY: Do you believe in mercy? What have you done in your long "service" to the State that was a human act.
ANN: I've done this. *(Pause)* They'll take you back to your cell.

END

DAVID MAMET's numerous plays include *Oleanna, Glengarry Glen Ross* (winner of the Pulitzer Prize and New York Drama Critics' Circle Award), *American Buffalo, Speed-the-Plow, Boston Marriage, November* and *Race*. He wrote the screenplays for such films as *The Verdict, The Untouchables* and *Wag the Dog*, and has twice been nominated for an Academy Award. He has written and directed ten films, including *Homicide, The Spanish Prisoner, State and Main, House of Games, Spartan* and *Redbelt*. In addition, he wrote the novels *The Village, The Old Religion, Wilson* and many books of nonfiction, including *Bambi vs. Godzilla: On the Nature, Purpose and Practice of the Movie Business; Theatre; Three Uses of the Knife: On the Nature and Purpose of Drama* and the *New York Times* bestseller *The Secret Knowledge: On the Dismantling of American Culture*. His HBO film *Phil Spector*, starring Al Pacino and Helen Mirren, will air in 2013. He was co-creator and executive producer of the CBS television show *The Unit* and is a founding member of the Atlantic Theater Company.